Make a New Friend in Jesus

PassAlong Arch® Books help you share Jesus with friends close to you and with children all around the world!

When you've enjoyed this story, pass it along to a friend. When your friend is finished, mail this book to the address below. Concordia Gospel Outreach promises to deliver your book to a boy or girl somewhere in the world to help him or her learn about Jesus.

Myself

My name _____

My address _____

_____

My PassAlong Friend

My name _____

My address _____

_____

When you're ready to give your PassAlong Arch® Book to a new friend who doesn't know about Jesus, mail it to

Concordia Gospel Outreach
3547 Indiana Avenue
St. Louis, MO 63118

PassAlong Series

God's Good Creation
Noah's Floating Zoo
Jesus Stills the Storm
God's Easter Plan

Copyright© 1994 Concordia Publishing House
3558 S. Jefferson Avenue, St. Louis, MO 63118-3968
Manufactured in the United States of America

1 2 3 4 5 6 7 8 9 10   03 02 01 00 99 98 97 96 95 94

Jesus
Stills the Storm

Mark 4:35–41 for Children

Carol Greene
Illustrated by Michelle Dorenkamp

ST. LOUIS

Day by day, day by day,
Jesus taught the crowds God's way.
"God's kingdom is like this," He'd say,
Day by day, day by day.

"I wonder what Jesus taught."

"What a crowd!"

One sunny day upon the shore,
The ground was packed with
folks galore.
So from a boat He taught some more,
One sunny day upon the shore.

Now, Jesus told fine tales indeed
   Of good plump corn and prickly weed,
   Of glowing lamp and mustard seed.
   Yes, Jesus told fine tales indeed.

   And each tale helped the people see
   How full of faith their lives could be,
   How full of hope and charity.
   Each tale helped the people see.

"I don't like prickly weeds."

Then evening came to end the day
And He felt He must get away
To be alone and rest and pray,
As evening came to end the day.

"Jesus worked hard today."

The lake was deep, the lake was wide.
Jesus took His friends aside.
"Please sail across and let Me ride."
The lake was deep, the lake was wide.

"Sometimes we call this lake the Sea of Galilee."

In the boat, He closed His eyes.
   He didn't see the dark clouds rise
   And churn across the evening skies.
   In the boat, He closed His eyes.

"WOW! Look at those clouds!"

His friends all felt a pang of fear.
"It's going to squall." "A storm is near."
"Get ready now. It's almost here!"
His friends all felt a pang of fear.

"A squall is a pretty nasty storm."

And then the wind began to blow.
It tossed that poor boat to and fro.
It tossed it high. It tossed it low.
The wind, the wind began to blow.

"Good Grief!"

The rain came down in sheets and showers.
The waves rose up in peaks and towers.
It seemed to last for hours and hours.
The rain came down in sheets and showers.

"Whee!"

The lake was wide, the lake was deep.
Death rode on those waves so steep.
But Jesus still lay fast asleep.
The lake was wide, the lake was deep.

W hen it grew too much to bear,
His friends cried out, "Oh, Lord, beware!
We're going to sink, Lord,
    don't You care?"
It had grown too much to bear.

"What will Jesus do?"

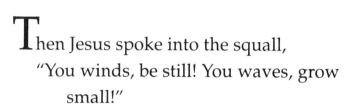

Then Jesus spoke into the squall,
  "You winds, be still! You waves, grow
    small!"
  At once there was no sound at all,
  For Jesus spoke into the squall.

"It's a miracle!"

He asked His friends with eyes so sad,
  "Why were you scared? I thought
      you had
  More faith in Me." Then they felt bad,
  Because He asked with eyes so sad.

"They didn't learn
what Jesus taught."

And yet each heart with wonder filled.
"Who is this Man? The storm He stilled.
The wind and waves did what He willed."
Oh, how each heart with wonder filled.